I CAN.
I WILL.
WATCH
ME.

I CAN. I WILL. WATCH ME

How to Not Be Overlooked, Underpaid, or Undervalued

Copyright © 2022 by Arika L Pierce.

ISBN: 9798425206022

Cover Photography by Andre Williams of ICUDMV Photography

Edited by Ethleen Sawyerr of Speak Write Play, LLC and Adeyinka Pierce-Watkins

I CAN.
I WILL.
WATCH
ME.

HOW TO NOT BE OVERLOOKED, UNDERPAID, OR UNDERVALUED

ARIKA L. PIERCE

CONTENTS

YOU MUST BE SEEN TO
ADVANCE YOUR
CAREER.
YOU MUST HAVE A
PLAN TO BE PAID AND
PROMOTED,
AND YOU MUST BE
VALUED TO ELEVATE
TO THE NEXT LEVEL.

INTRODUCTION

If you are reading this book, I trust that you want more out of your career. Most of the professionals that I work with and come across are all ambitious (or they wouldn't seek me out). But something you will read throughout this book is that ambition alone is not enough when it comes to your career; you must also have a strategy.

As a leadership coach and founder of a professional development community called The Millennial Boardroom, I've spoken to thousands of professionals who are unhappy with where they are in their careers. As I thought about a book that I could write to address some of the common challenges I heard, I landed here. **You must be seen to advance your career. You must have a plan to be paid and promoted, and you must be valued to elevate to the next level.** In each part of this book, I will take you through the exact steps to overcome these challenges and face the fears you have about your career. I'm thrilled to share these proven techniques, and I hope you feel excited to implement them.

This book is hands-on and geared to the person who is ready to gain control of their career and take immediate action to be seen, paid, promoted, and valued. As you go through this book, don't try to take shortcuts by skipping some of the steps. Think of this book as a roadmap; the destination and route must come from you. This book has a lot of information that I am confident can change the trajectory of your career, but you have to do the work to see the results.

Also, to help you take action, I have created a complimentary toolkit available for download from my website at www.arikapierce.com/booktoolkit.

Now let's get to work!

"I'M NOT READY" IS A LIE.

PART ONE

BE SEEN

Definition of *overlooked:*
not seen, noticed, or considered

This section will focus on tactics to ensure you are not invisible at work and end up missing out on or not being considered for growth and advancement opportunities.

Does any of this sound familiar?

- Your work is not acknowledged or recognized
- No one at work ever seeks out your opinions or ideas
- When you express your opinions or ideas, they are ignored
- You aren't included on projects or in meetings where your expertise would be useful

When the pandemic first hit in March 2020 and many employees moved from being in-person office workers to remote workers, one of the phrases I heard the most was, "I'm just going to do my job and stay under the radar." This might have been an okay strategy for the first few months while everyone was trying to figure out how to adjust to an all-remote environment, but I can tell you that one of the biggest mistakes you can make in your career is staying under the radar.

If you are not "seen" by key stakeholders in your company, I can almost promise you that your career will not advance. People who are invisible will not get the same opportunities as those who are "known" and make a name for themselves. For some people, showing up and being seen is easy. They always have something to say (even when that something is nothing), and their names seem to always come up in conversations and dialogues ("Was Kristen invited to this meeting? She always has such good input and asks poignant questions.") For others, being seen is a challenge. Perhaps you are new in your organization, shy, or just can't figure out how to get your voice in the mix. Well, this section of the book is for both of these types of people. Even if you are comfortable speaking up, having a <u>visibility strategy</u> is more than just asking a lot of questions in team meetings and having a good relationship with your boss. In this section, I will help you shape your visibility strategy so that you are not the best-kept secret in your organization.

CHAPTER 1

Mindset: Do You See You?

Before we jump into creating your visibility strategy, I first want you to spend some time evaluating how you see yourself. For a lot of the professionals that I work with, their biggest block in moving forward is themselves. They can't get past thinking they are not ready for new opportunities or growth, so they keep quiet and look for validation from others that they are on a career growth trajectory instead. Remember these four words: **"READY" IS A LIE.** Stop talking yourself out of not knowing enough or not having enough experience. You are the CEO of Me, Inc., which means you need to embrace owning and marketing who you are professionally.

Let's start with a journaling exercise. I'm old school, so I always recommend putting pen to paper. But if you would rather journal on your computer or in the Notes app on your phone, that's fine. Commit to answering these questions without any interruptions. I suggest setting a timer or the alarm on your phone (or perhaps Alexa) and letting the first thoughts that come to mind flow out of you. Don't worry about sentence formation or correct grammar; no one will be reviewing this but you.

The Questions

1. Who are you currently professionally? (This is not your job title or company name, but it is a deeper answer into who you are as a professional.)
2. How did you get here?
3. How do others see you?
4. How would others describe you professionally?
5. How do you want to be seen or described?

Ok, set the timer *now* and give your honest answers to these questions. Don't hold back and don't autocorrect yourself. Let what comes to mind flow onto your paper or computer screen.

I recently had the members of The Millennial Boardroom do this exercise, and the responses were fascinating. Some people struggled to define who they were professionally without referencing their job titles or positions. Many said, "I have no idea" or "I never really thought about who I was professionally." One person wrote about his leadership skills:

> I am an authentic and collaborative leader who has had roles of significant responsibility within the consumer goods industry, and what makes me different is my ability to build relationships with my customers

> and with people. The key to my success has been my ability to get to know people and know what makes them tick and easily build trust.

He was so unapologetic about who he was professionally that it was clear that he knew how he wanted to be seen by others.

Many people never really stop to self-reflect when it comes to their careers and who they are, which is the reason for these questions. These people may aspire to get promoted or receive a raise, but they have not spent time thinking about who they are professionally beyond their job titles and who they want to be. Here's the thing, if you want to stop being overlooked and be seen, you have to first think about how you see yourself.

When I was in my corporate career, I wanted to always be seen as someone who could think strategically and add big-picture value to meetings and projects. As a result, my last corporate position (before I left to become a full-time Leadership Coach) was the Senior Vice President of Strategy and Growth. I became known as someone who could look beyond the day-to-day operations of the company I worked for and think long-term about what it would take to grow the company by X percent or in X years. When I was in meetings, I consistently looked for ways to ask questions a little differently from everyone else, and I always did my research so that I understood industry trends and changes.

These specific tactics identified me as a big-picture thinker, and this quality became one of my leadership superpowers.

Now, back to you. How do you want to be seen? Are you seen as a junior employee who is comfortable doing low-priority tasks or a key leader who is ready and capable of taking on more?

LEADERSHIP IS AN ACTION, NOT A TITLE OR POSITION OR YOUR PLACE ON THE ORG CHART

If you want to advance in your career, you must be *seen and experienced* as a leader. Many people struggle with this, and I often hear people say, "Well, I'm not a leader yet." I respond by explaining that leadership is not about a title or position on an organizational chart. Leadership is a verb; it is an action. If you are influencing, motivating, and engaging others, you are leading. I'm going to guess that if you don't see yourself as a leader (yet), it's because you are probably hiding your leadership strengths or waiting on someone else to invite you to be seen as one. I want to challenge you to recognize and see yourself as a leader in your organization today so that key stakeholders will see it in you as well. This is what will allow you to seize new opportunities.

Here is your next action assignment. Over the next few days, I want you to observe yourself at work. Each day, take ten minutes to journal your observations by asking yourself the following questions:

1. In my interactions today with my boss, team members, colleagues, etc., did I make an impact?
2. Did I commit any acts of leadership today?
3. How was I "seen" and experienced by others today?

After doing this for three to four days, you will likely start to see some patterns. Perhaps you will realize that you make more of an impact than you thought or that you do not do enough things to demonstrate your leadership skills. Perhaps you will uncover some leadership abilities that have been hidden, such as thinking strategically or listening to understand. Or maybe you will realize that you often shy away from revealing your leadership strengths. And lastly, maybe you will receive feedback while doing the exercise that will confirm that you are seen as a key member of your organization (the lack of feedback may confirm that your talents and strengths are a secret within your organization).

These questions and exercises are really meant to shift your thinking to a growth mindset where you are ready to do the work, take action, and own how you show up and are seen. Unless you take these steps, it will be difficult to design a successful visibility strategy that will propel you to being someone who immediately comes to mind for career advancement opportunities. As I stated earlier, mindset is what usually holds many of us back when it comes to career growth. It's difficult to be seen if you don't even believe that you should be in the meeting or on the team. This is more than just having confidence; it's about truly seeing yourself as a valuable leader in higher-level positions and doing what it takes so that others see you as a person who is ready for those types of opportunities. Yes, there are tactical steps you will need to take. We will spend most of this book covering those actions, but I would be doing you a disservice if I didn't first challenge you to think inwardly and do a little digging around to determine what you think of yourself professionally. If you are reading this book, I have to assume you are someone who doesn't want to dim their light or play small. If you want to stop being overlooked for career growth opportunities, then you must shift to a growth mindset first. Here are ten ways to do this:

1. **Embrace failure**—failure is one of the stops on the way to success.
2. **Be curious**—never stop learning. When you stop learning, you stop leading.
3. **Have a can-do attitude**—remember, "ready" is a lie!
4. **Challenge yourself**—the only way to grow is to stretch yourself through challenges.
5. **Be open to changes**—growth begins when you step outside of your comfort zone.
6. **Set goals**—the only way for your mind to move forward is to be clear about the goals you are moving toward.

7. **Show grit**—fostering grit can help you move forward and be focused on your goals, even if there are obstacles you have to face along the way.
8. **Welcome feedback**—listen to feedback, then adjust and grow.
9. **Exercise mindfulness**—learn ways to focus and clear your mind.
10. **Add "yet" to your vocabulary**—this helps you overcome anything despite any challenges or struggles you face.

So, I want to ask you again: How do you want to be seen professionally? Now, start to think about what might be holding you back from being seen this way. Are you committed to doing your part to not being overlooked and discovering what role you may play in being invisible? As a black woman who worked for fifteen years in corporate America, I understand that workplace dynamics, such as the "old boys club," can be challenging to break into. But I also know that sometimes it's easier for us to blame everyone else except ourselves for why we are "not seen." I want to help you focus on the things that *are* within your control when it comes to your visibility strategy and tactically create a plan to become unstoppable!

It's time to focus on what will get you to the next level in your career and a seat at the leadership table. I want you to say it with me: "I'm not ready" is a LIE!

IF YOU ARE ONLY
FOCUSED ON BEING
VISIBLE AND "SEEN"
BY YOUR BOSS, YOUR
STRATEGY
WILL FALL SHORT.

CHAPTER 2

Who Needs to See You?

Okay, it's time to get tactical. Many professionals get serious about being more visible, then focus solely on the relationship they have with their bosses—BIG MISTAKE. Your boss is one person in the hemisphere of stakeholders. While they do have some control over your career opportunities and growth, they are not the end-all-be-all. Should you nurture this relationship? Absolutely! But if you are only focused on being visible and "seen" by your boss, your strategy will fall short. Your boss has their own priorities; while a good boss will want to see their employee excel, they are also likely focused on their own agenda. Also, I've seen it time and time again where a boss moves on to a new role, new company, or (gasp) is fired, and all their direct reports are nervous because they don't have close connections with other people in the organization. Essentially, you don't want to be in a scenario where your boss leaves the company or goes to a different department, leaving you without any other strong relationships with key stakeholders in your company. There are also situations in which your boss isn't always well-liked or is seen by others as difficult to get along with. Do you want to be seen the same way just because you report to that person, or do you want to own how other key stakeholders see you? If it's the latter, get out your notebook again so that we can get to work.

You need to create a visibility stakeholder analysis, then assess which stakeholders need to see you so that you advance in your career. Don't skip over this step because you may waste time focusing your visibility strategy on the wrong people. I will walk you step by step on how to do this:

1. Make a list of all (and I mean *all*) of the people who have an interest in your career success or failure, as well as those who are impacted by your role.
2. Classify each person on the list as follows:
   a. Stakeholders with low interest in your career success and low influence over your career success.
   b. Stakeholders with low interest in your career success and high influence in your career success.
   c. Stakeholders with high interest in your career success and low influence in your career success.
   d. Stakeholders with high interest in your career success and high influence in your career success.

3. Download the stakeholder analysis map on the next page at www.arikapierce.com/booktoolkit
4. Plot each person on the map based on their power and influence levels.
5. Analyze!

Stakeholder Analysis Map

STAY ON THE RADAR   ACTIVE VISIBILITY

MONITOR   KEEP INFORMED

1. STAKEHOLDERS WITH HIGH INTEREST AND HIGH INFLUENCE = Active Visibility

These are the stakeholders who can make or break your career. They not only have a great deal of interest in the success or failure of your career, but they also have a lot of influence in determining your success or failure. The visibility strategy for this group is to be actively engaged with them consistently and exceed their expectations. These are the people who need to know you are a superstar!

Regularly communicate with these stakeholders and inform them of your accomplishments and career aspirations. Building strong relationships with these stakeholders is crucial, so it is important to gain their trust and support. This group typically has a lot of influence within the organization. With their formal influence, they can help you. Try to turn these stakeholders into your ambassadors. You want them to always be armed with positive information about you so that they can speak highly about you even when you are not in the room.

The stakeholder group with high interest and high influence is the most important group; therefore, be self-critical of who you put in this quadrant. One common mistake is to put too many stakeholders in this quadrant. It is not impossible to have many stakeholders with high interest and influence, but the more individuals you classify as "active visibility," the busier you will be. Force yourself to select the top three or top five. Start working intensively together with these three to five stakeholders (your key stakeholders) on conveying your value and results, showcasing your leadership actions, and most importantly, your longer-term career goals.

2. STAKEHOLDERS WITH LOW INTEREST AND HIGH INFLUENCE = Stay on the Radar

This stakeholder group does not have as much interest, either positive or negative, in your career success. However, these stakeholders have a lot of influence. The management strategy for this group is to stay on the radar and make sure you are meeting their needs, but you don't need to spend as much time with them.

In order to effectively manage stakeholders with low interest and high influence, you must primarily keep them informed about the things you are doing that matter most to them. Perhaps these are team members with whom you are working on a special project or members or senior members from a different department with whom you have to collaborate. Many people find this stakeholder group to be the most difficult to manage. To be fair, being able to manage this group effectively requires some political skills. It is also good to be aware that this group of people can help you increase the breadth of your visibility. If you keep these stakeholders satisfied, you will create a name for yourself outside of your core network. Immerse yourself in their motives. Get to know their interests. Understand what they want and need to achieve to become successful themselves and find out what they are being "judged on." With these insights, you can inform, help, and ultimately engage with them more effectively to stay on their radar.

3. STAKEHOLDERS WITH HIGH INTEREST AND LOW INFLUENCE = Keep Informed

These stakeholders have high interest in your career success but low influence to intervene or change things. The stakeholder management strategy for this group is to keep them informed. For many people, these stakeholders may be consulting partners or support staff. Your goal with this group is to communicate and engage with them so that no major issues arise. For example, the stakeholders in this category can often be helpful in ensuring a project you are working on runs smoothly. A key piece of advice here is to interact with this group at times when it suits you and discuss areas that are important to you. Maintaining this balance prevents a group of stakeholders with little influence from determining your agenda and consuming your time.

4. STAKEHOLDERS WITH LOW INTEREST AND LOW INFLUENCE = Monitor

Let me first be clear by saying "monitor" doesn't mean "ignore!" While this group of people has little interest in your career and success, you want to keep an eye on these stakeholders and occasionally evaluate if any changes have occurred. It is possible that people in this group may shift to one of the other stakeholder groups, for example, because of a promotion or reorganization. Through such events, they may gain more interest or influence, which will make these stakeholders more important. Since this stakeholder group has low interest and low influence, limit your time spent on them.

I know this process can seem a bit overwhelming, so I want to share a real example of how I did this analysis with one of the members of The Millennial Boardroom community. Let's call her Melissa.

Melissa is a sales rep for a midsize technology company. She is responsible for acquiring, leading, and developing sales opportunities in her assigned territory. I had Melissa make a list of everyone who had an interest in the success or failure of her role as a sales rep or could impact (or be impacted by) her role.

It took her some time to create the list, but here is what she came up with (she listed people in no specific order of priority).

- My boss
- VP sales
- Colleagues
- Lead generation
- Consultants
- Consultants' admin
- Sales admin/support
- HR director
- Non-sales operations
- IT support
- Marketing coordinator
- Contracts/legal
- C-suite
- Finance director
- Service sales
- Director renewals
- Partner sales

Next, Melissa went through the list. For each person, she decided if they had a high or low level of power (or influence) and whether their level of interest in her success was low or high. She then wrote the name of each person in the appropriate quadrant that matched their power and interest.

Melissa's Analysis

Ok, so here's the fun part. These were Melissa's key take-aways from the analysis:

Active visibility. Melissa wasn't surprised about the people that she needed to actively stay visible with, but she did realize that she overly relied on having a strong relationship with her boss. Instead, she needed to look for opportunities to be visible to her boss' boss—the VP of sales. I asked Melissa if the VP of sales ever did "skip-level meetings," which are held between a manager's manager and their employees. She wasn't sure, so I suggested that she consider requesting one with the VP of sales to develop a stronger relationship, learn more about strategic initiatives happening at her company, and gain insights into the VP's own priorities and goals. Bottom line: The more you are visible, known, and respected by people above you, the better off you are from a career standpoint. Melissa wasn't familiar with the concept of a skip-level meeting and was a little nervous about "going over her boss." This may be the case for you, so here's a brief overview of what a skip-level meeting is and why it's needed for a visibility strategy.

Skip-Level Meetings

What are they? They are essentially meetings with your boss' boss without your boss being present. For example, let's say the VP of sales has four managers who report to him or her. A skip-level meeting would occur when the VP of sales meets with the direct reports of his or her four managers.

Why do they happen? Skip-level meetings are an important management tool and should not be received as negative or going over your boss' head. The goal should be to maintain and increase communication so that all parties learn more about what's happening in the organization from each perspective. Also, skip-level meetings offer opportunities to develop professional relationships, especially if you don't have regular interactions with senior management.

How do I schedule one? A good leader schedules skip-level meetings periodically with their team. But it should come as no surprise that many leaders don't always check in with their broader team members or make it a priority. If skip-level meetings are not part of your organization's culture, you should consider reaching out to senior managers on your own (but do run it past your boss first and explain why you would like to have the opportunity to meet with their boss). Some bosses might push back on this, but theoretically, they should not prevent you from requesting a skip-level meeting with their boss. Once you have spoken with your boss, here is a sample email you can send to your boss' boss. Please adapt it to fit your scenario:

Hi [Skip-Level Boss' First Name],

My name is [Your First Name], and I work with [Your Boss' Name] as [Your Title]. If possible, I'd like to schedule 30 minutes to learn more about your role at [Company Name]. I'd love to hear more about your journey and see if you have any tips on my career growth.

When you have an opportunity, could you share your availability over the next few weeks, or can I work with [Skip-Level Boss' Admin's Name] to schedule time with you?

Thank you,
[Your First Name]

What happens during the meeting? First, keep in mind that *you* requested the meeting. Even though this is your boss' boss, it is your responsibility to properly prepare for the meeting and come up with thoughtful questions and discussion topics. A skip-level meeting is *not* the time to critique or give feedback about your boss. It is also not the time to discuss salary, promotions, or additional responsibilities. Remember, the topics you discuss with your boss' boss will most likely go back to your boss. Don't say anything you don't want to get back to your boss.

So, what DO you talk about? Here are some sample questions to ask. Feel free to make changes so it makes sense for you and your organization. (Actually, absolutely make changes.)

Team Alignment

1. What are your goals for the department this quarter? This year? Five years from now? How do you think we are going to reach those goals?
2. What do you consider to be our team's top priorities for this year?
3. How can our team provide more meaningful contributions to the company?
4. What one thing should our team work to improve?

Company Growth

1. How do you see the company developing in the next three years?
2. What initiatives are being considered this year?
3. Which competitors are you most concerned about?
4. What industry trends concern or excite you?

Professional Growth

1. How did your career develop at this company?
2. What should I focus on at this point in my career?
3. What skills am I missing if I want to advance?
4. What one thing would you tell your younger self about career advancement?

Another insightful question to ask: What is demanding or consuming most of your time right now? This is a great way to get information on the skip-level boss' top priorities in the organization.

What happens after the meeting? Always send a follow-up note after the meeting to thank the skip-level boss for their time. And if you said you would follow up on something, make sure you do. Also, consider asking for a quarterly meeting and getting it on the calendar as soon as possible.

Ok, back to Melissa and her analysis.

Stay on the radar. Melissa realized that there were some key people in the low-interest-high-influence box that she needed to have a closer relationship with. For example, her regional sales manager is a critical player in her success as a sales rep because they help to close deals with new clients. Instead of just relying on email to communicate about their sales pipeline, Melissa decided more face-to-face time was needed to develop a rapport. This way, she could more easily call on the sales manager when a deal was on the line. Her action item here was to set up a casual monthly lunch.

Keep informed. For this category, Melissa felt like she had the right level of visibility. For example, while partner sales reps show a lot of interest by being in touch frequently with Melissa, they don't have that much power over her career success.

Monitor. In this category, Melissa noticed that she had weekly one-hour meetings with the consulting admin to review sales opportunities. While this meeting is important, it takes a lot of time. After analyzing the interest and influence levels, Melissa decided to change them to bi-weekly thirty-minute meetings.

Before you move on to the next chapter, I want you to do your own analysis. While it may seem a little painful, it will be incredibly insightful as you think about who needs to *see* you and, frankly, who doesn't.

JUST
BEING GOOD AT
YOUR
JOB ISN'T WHAT
GETS
YOU PROMOTED.

CHAPTER 3

Open Your Door and Knock on a Few

A promotion opportunity recently came up in Jay's department. The job perfectly matched Jay's skills and experience, so he was sure he would be selected for the role. In the end, Jay didn't even get an interview, and even more shocking to Jay, the person who was selected for the promotion had less experience. Jay went to his boss to ask why he wasn't even considered for the role. His boss said that, other than herself, no one else on the selection panel knew who Jay was, so she couldn't make the case that Jay was the right person for the job. While the person who was ultimately selected had less experience than Jay, she had built some strong connections with key stakeholders within the company and had even represented the department at company-wide events. As a result, the selection panel had more confidence that she was a better fit for the role than Jay.

TIP: Don't be Jay.

Ever heard of this scenario? I know, I know, it's not fair. If you are good at your job, that should be enough. Well, if you have worked over three days in the professional world, you should know that just being good at your job isn't what always gets you promoted. In his book, Empowering Yourself: The Organizational Game Revealed, Harvey Coleman states that career success is based on three key elements: performance, image, and exposure (aka PIE):

1. **Performance**: This is about the day-to-day work you're tasked with and the quality of the results you deliver.
2. **Image**: This is what other people think of you—your personal brand. Do you maintain a positive attitude? Do you lead with solutions to issues, or are you the sole person who offers roadblocks when others suggest changes or alternatives?
3. **Exposure**: Who knows about you and what you do? Does your boss know what you do? Does their boss know you and what you do? Do others inside and outside your organization know anything about you?

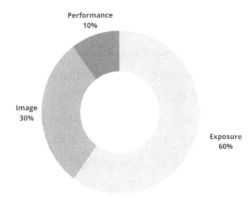

Although Coleman's book was published way back in 1996, the implications referenced still ring true today. If all you do is perform your job well, then you'll probably get some form of pay raise or bonus, which is perfectly okay for some people. However, if you want a promotion, you'll need to perform well, cultivate a positive image, and pro-actively gain exposure to a broad array of "right" stake-holders.

So, how exactly do you gain more "exposure" at work when you are behind a computer all day? What if you, like many of us currently, work remotely? This can be even more challenging. In this chapter, I am going to break down twenty-seven exposure activities. Do you need to do them all? Of course not. And quite frankly, I hope you are already doing some of them. The goal here is to give you some actionable tactics that can get you to that 60% exposure piece of the PIE!

1. **Speak up in meetings.** I think most people would agree that the easiest way to make yourself visible is to be seen and heard more. Easy enough, right? Well, yes and no. You don't want to become the person known for just talking for the sake of hearing himself or herself speak, nor do you want to be someone who just repeats what their team members say or chimes in to agree with the boss. You *want* to become known as someone who always brings their intellectual capital to meetings and discussions. This means you show up prepared to be engaged, ask killer questions, and challenge points appropriately. If you are holding the meeting, you are organized and structured; it's clear you are confident about the information you are presenting. The bottom line is that you want to add value when you speak up, and the only way to do that is through being prepared and offering your intellectual capital. Look at your calendar for the upcoming week and identify the value that you can add to each meeting or discussion. If you are asked to be in the meeting to listen only, respect this request, but look for other ways to share key information after the meeting.

   TIP: Avoid a brain blank in the middle of a meeting by writing down the key points you want to make and listing the questions you want to ask in advance.

2. **Show up early to meetings, not on time.** This is another tactic that may seem obvious. Keep reading because there is a strategy for this. When you show up early for

meetings, you have the chance to make small talk with other attendees; this is key for a visibility strategy. Yes, sometimes it can be painful talking about the weather ad nauseam, but it can also lead to finding out what projects a key stakeholder is working on that perhaps you wouldn't otherwise know about. It could also result in building a rapport with some of the people you've identified as having influence over the success of your career. I made a point of always doing this when I worked in corporate America, and it allowed me to forge some strategic relationships outside of my core day-to-day team.

TIP: If making small talk is difficult for you, prepare in advance a number of open-ended questions that you can use to start conversations.

3. **Be positive**. There's a popular saying that people won't always remember what you said, but they will remember how you made them feel. This stands true at work. Everyone is human, and people will remember and "see" you more if they have good experiences with you. Always be positive, give compliments, and acknowledge the accomplishments of others. Sometimes, we are so busy that we forget how positivity and being nice to others (skills we learned in pre-school and kindergarten) can help fuel our career growth.

TIP: Make it a point to have at least one "positive" communication with your active visibility stakeholders each week.

4. **Volunteer for high-visibility projects**. Do a quick survey of your current workload. Are you working on any project or doing anything that promotes your visibility outside of your boss and core team? If the answer is "no," then start looking for high-visibility projects that you can help support and advance within your organization. I recall celebrating my former company's 30th anniversary. Members of the planning committee were looking for volunteers to lead sessions that took employees through the history of the company in a game-like fashion. It required training and committing to doing a few sessions every week, but it was a great visibility project because every employee at every level had to attend a session. Honestly, was it something I wanted to do? No. But it was a project that was a priority of the C-suite (executive-level management) and made me visible to other people in the company, so I jumped at the opportunity.

5. **Request more responsibilities.** Let me give you some advice, don't ever tell your boss that you are bored. If you find yourself in a place where you aren't challenged and would like to increase your level of responsibilities, then you need to ask for more duties appropriately. As a former boss of a large team, if I had an employee who was doing their job well, unless they

told me otherwise, I assumed their workload was appropriate. It's up to you to let your boss know you are ready for more, and it's also up to you to know if you can take on more or are just trying to move up. Know the difference. If it's the former, have a conversation with your boss about how to adjust your workload so you can take on more responsibilities. If it's the latter, think about how you can optimize some of your existing workload to make your contribution more valuable.

6. **Research solutions to long-standing problems.** In general, most people are good at uncovering or pointing out a problem, but few people are problem solvers. Trust me, you want to be a problem solver, not the problem pointer-outer. Look around your organization and identify some problems or challenges, then think of ways you can help solve them.

I recently challenged members of The Millennial Boardroom community to do this, and we had a lot of fun with it. Many members were proactive and took some ideas back to their organizations. For example, one of the members shared that a lot of people were complaining about the onboarding process for new employees because everyone in her company worked remotely. Even though she worked in marketing, she came up with a few ideas to smooth out the process so that new employees felt more welcomed in their first few days. She ended up reaching out to HR to share her ideas and offering to lead an onboarding ambassador program. It was successful, and she later received an email from the president of her company thanking her for taking the initiative to make new employees feel more welcome. Another member noticed that their company blog was stale and shared some topic ideas and even authored a blog once a month. This allowed her to position herself as a thought leader in the organization and later led to her being asked to represent the company at their industry conference.

TIP: You don't have to always look for big problems to solve—small problems need solving, too—just make sure it's a problem that will be of value to your organization.

7. **Participate in work-related activities**. I know, I know, most people want to leave work at work. I get it. But organizations spend a lot of time and money on activities to promote employee engagement and maintain a more cohesive company culture. Prioritize participating in these activities by attending lunch-and-learns, company volunteer activities, and other work-related events. Be a good sport and encourage your other team members to engage as well. We all have busy lives, so attending everything is not always possible. Participating in these types of events helps with visibility and conveys that you are a part of the organization, not just a worker bee. And guess what? You might end up having a little fun in the process.

8. **Volunteer to represent your team.** Take things to the next level beyond just participating in work-related activities. When there is an opportunity, look for ways to represent your team. This is a great way to showcase yourself as a leader. Perhaps there is a monthly company meeting and your team needs a representative to attend and report back, or maybe there is an upcoming conference and your boss asks for volunteers to attend and/or "man the exhibit booth." Again, while this may not be exactly how you want to spend your time outside of work, these are fantastic visibility opportunities.

Early in my career, I volunteered to attend a major conference for my company and work shifts in the booth to distribute our marketing materials and tchotchkes (it was mindless work). Well, do you know what happened? The senior executives who were at the conference invited me to dinner with them during the conference, and I got valuable face time (and a fancy dinner) with key stakeholders in my company.

9. **Build a network with colleagues outside of your team.** The previous example is one way I started to network with colleagues outside of my core team, and it significantly helped with my visibility strategy. As I shared in the last chapter, don't make the mistake of thinking that being known by your boss or liked by your team is enough to get you promoted and to the next level. In your organization, networking internally is just as important as networking externally. I've seen many

companies do reorganizations and bosses or whole teams leave unexpectedly, so always be prepared for that. Who else outside of your team knows you and your work within your organization? If that list is short, you need to start doing something about it.

10. **Establish an effective communication channel with your boss**. Your boss is not the end-all-be-all when it comes to your visibility. With that said, you do need to ensure that you have an effective communication channel with your boss. I am a big fan of dedicated, weekly one-on-one meetings. I often hear people say, "I talk to or email with my boss at some point every day, so I don't need to have a weekly scheduled meeting with them." I disagree. A weekly one-on-one is not just a time for you to give an update on what you are working on; it is a strategic opportunity to ensure your work is aligned with your boss' goals. It's an opportunity to share accomplishments, ask strategic, big-picture questions, and develop a rapport with your boss.

In my corporate career, I always found these meetings incredibly valuable and went to them prepared with items I wanted to speak with my boss about or get more clarity or direction on. In my last corporate role, I reported to the CEO of the company. While I had multiple meetings with her and others throughout the week, I used our one-on-one meetings to get to know her better and find out more about how I could support her success as the leader of the company.

11. Thought leadership. How much do you know about the industry you are working in? Are you tracking trends? Changes? Competitor activity? If you want to be visible, position yourself as a thought leader. I think the easiest way to do this is by stepping up your LinkedIn game. Are you connected and following some of the leaders in your organization and industry as a whole? What are they posting about? What articles are they reading? Jump into the conversation—share your thoughts and opinions (I would be careful about getting too radical, but I leave you to your own professional judgment). Does your company have a blog, podcast, or regular webinar session? Check it out and reshare the content. If it's appropriate, you can even volunteer to help with some of these activities.

In 2010, I worked at a healthcare company during the passage of the healthcare reform legislation. One of the ways I became visible in the company was by sharing summaries that explained some of the law changes and their impact on our company and clients. I know thought leadership can seem scary and overwhelming, but it doesn't have to be. Start with sharing one or two new articles on LinkedIn that are relevant to your industry and adding a sentence or two of commentary. Here, I'll get you started: Check out this article on [Insert Article Link]! It gives some great insights on [List Relevant Topic(s)]. How do you think this will impact the industry?

12. **Participate in learning opportunities.** If your company offers any learning or professional development opportunities, say "yes" to attending every time. Don't ever think that you are too seasoned to learn something new or that it's not a good use of your time. The people who take advantage of these opportunities are usually the ones who get noticed and get ahead faster. It also means your organization is willing to invest in you, and to say "no" sends a bad message that you are not interested in your own development. I always found these opportunities to be good ways to get to know other people and develop new relationships because there was usually a mix of different people from within the company present.

13. **Build your expertise to become known and recognized.** We will dive deeper into this in Part Three of the book when we focus on your value. For now, just know part of being more visible and not undervalued is building your expertise. What exactly is it that you are known for and recognized as? I know it's not an easy question to answer. Later, we will discuss much deeper the process to determine your "brand value." For now, just know it's an important tactic to identify what you want to be visible for and then create opportunities to showcase this skill.

14. **Regularly update your accomplishments list**. Do you have a brag list or a list of your accomplishments? I don't mean a list in your head or bullet points on your resume. I mean a list in an actual notebook, Word

document, or Notes app in your phone that you update regularly with notable accomplishments (big and small). I'll tell you a secret, no one cares about your career as much as you do. Unlike with professional athletes, no one is likely keeping track of your "stats" if you are not. This is a critical list because most of us suffer from "recency syndrome" and can only recall things that happened recently.

> **TIP**: At the end of each week, review the meetings, appointments, and projects you were involved in, then summarize your accomplishments in two to three concise bullet points.

15. **Get feedback.** If you are unclear about how you are seen, one of the easiest ways to find out is to ask. I know that it might seem uncomfortable, but just asking your boss or a trusted colleague about their perception of you at work and/or if they have any suggestions on how you can gain greater visibility can go a long way. It will save you from wasting time on the wrong exposure activities.

16. **Ask what they are focused on and how you can help.** Look at the names of each person in the active visibility box of your stakeholder analysis. Remember, these are people who you want to stay front and center with. When was the last time you asked each person what they were focusing on and how you could help? These simple questions can go a long way. Posing them will

give you visibility and insight into your colleagues' work priorities and show that you have a genuine interest in knowing what is important to them.

17. **Be proactive by initiating next steps.** I hate when people say, "If you need some help, just let me know." It's basically putting it on the other person (who may already be overwhelmed and busy) to take action. If there is a high-visibility opportunity or project that you would like to be part of or work on, find a way to take action and insert yourself (appropriately). Recently, during my office hours in The Millennial Boardroom (every other Friday, members can stop by to ask me anything and get on-the-spot career coaching), a member came and said that her marketing firm had a new high-profile client. She hoped she would get selected to be on the team, but other than asking her boss, she didn't know how else to stand out. I suggested that she spend time doing some research about the client and come up with three to five ideas about how her firm could make the engagement a success. I told her to proactively send the ideas to her boss and/or schedule a time to review the suggestions. The objective was to show that she was already thinking about how the company could serve the client before she was even selected to be on the team. Guess what? Not only was she selected to work on the client's team, but she was also chosen to be one of the co-leaders.

18. **Find a sponsor.** A lot of people don't know the difference between a mentor and a sponsor, so here it is: a

mentor is someone you go to for advice and guidance. We all need mentors, and I am a firm believer that we need a diverse set of mentors for different areas of our lives—to challenge us and give us feedback. A sponsor is someone who advocates for you. Sponsors can use their influence and network to connect you to high-profile people, opportunities, pay raises, and promotions. A sponsor will be your champion and speak about you even when you are not in the room; they will use their own platforms and network for you to gain exposure. They also may connect you with opportunities that might not even be on your radar, which is why having a sponsor is vital for maximum visibility. See the difference? Now, if you don't have a sponsor, start thinking about how to secure one ASAP. But here is the key: you must "deliver the goods." This means your follow-through is critical; you don't want this person to take a risk on you and then let them down.

TIP: Want to learn more about career sponsorship? Watch Carla Harris's TED Talk: *"How to Find the Person Who Can Help You Get Ahead at Work."*

19. **Train and mentor others.** No matter your level at your organization, there is always someone to train or mentor. Think about some of your skills, then do an assessment of who could use your support or mentorship. I'm a big fan of reciprocal mentorship, where a senior-level employee partners with an entry or mid-level colleague to mentor each other. If you are highly skilled in

an area or knowledgeable about a tool that is more challenging to others, hold a lunch-and-learn and allow people to ask you questions. These types of opportunities are great displays of leadership visibility.

20. **Volunteer on the leadership team of a professional organization.** Identify a professional association that aligns with your industry and look for opportunities to be on the leadership team. Not only will this give you more visibility to industry stakeholders, but your organization will likely showcase you as you gain leadership experience.

7 Ways to Be More Visible in a Remote Environment

1. **Get on video.** I've been working remotely since 2015. In my last corporate role, I managed a team of individuals from all over the country, so video meetings are not new to me. I get that being on video is not always comfortable ("Zoom fatigue" is real), but guess what? The number one way to be visible in a remote environment is to turn the damn camera on. Even if you are the only one on camera, turn it on! Even if you are just there to listen, turn it on! Having your camera on at all times shows a level of professional maturity that is important for your visibility strategy. Show you are paying attention, add commentary to the chat, use the emoji feature (when appropriate), and of course, speak up and participate. Video meetings are not going away,

so having a strong executive presence digitally will be a key skill for the future of your professional career.

2. **Schedule more cross-departmental meetings.** One of the downsides of remote work is the lack of engagement with other teams. You no longer run into someone in the elevator or kitchen and have a quick, casual chat about what they are working on. This is key to visibility because, as I've shared before, only exposing yourself to your boss and team is not enough to advance in most organizations. Think about some of your other colleagues and set a goal to connect with someone different each week or every month. Be curious about their lives and work. Collaboration is always key in an organization, and many times, people are waiting for someone else to do it.

3. **Track and communicate your progress weekly.** As a former boss of a remote team, receiving weekly updates from my team was a critical way for me to stay up to date on their progress. I also sent my boss updates each week. Doing this doesn't have to be "more work" because it becomes an easier way to ensure you and your boss are aligned. To be one hundred percent honest, it shows your boss and others how hard you are working.

TIP: Keep the updates short and to the point.

Here is the template I used for my boss and team.

Hi [Boss' Name],

Priority Tasks and Projects This Week

- *Priority task #1*
- *Priority task #2*
- *Priority task #3*

Progress and Wins

- I finally [State accomplishment and its implication].
- It looks like [State progress made].

Looking forward to catching up at our next one-on-one meeting!

4. **Volunteer to sit in.** A major upside to remote work is that there may be opportunities for you to sit in on key meetings that you otherwise would not be a part of. For example, there might be a strategy, sales, or client status meeting in the office that you typically would not attend. Now that these meetings are virtual, ask your boss or other department leaders for opportunities to sit in so that you can listen to what's going on in other departments outside of your core areas. Many times, there is much to learn and leverage. Even though you won't be speaking during the meeting, the fact that you are "in the room" is great exposure.

5. **Proactively reach out.** Revisit your active visibility list. Create a schedule to share something your key

I CAN. I WILL. WATCH ME.

stakeholders would value. It could be an article, pod-cast episode, recent win, or congratulatory message.

> **TIP:** Include the key stakeholder's first name in the subject line to add a personal touch. It could say something like, "Hey Lindsey – this made me think of you!" This will make the recipient more likely to open your message immediately.

6. **Overcommunicate.** When you are working from home, there's no such thing as too much communication. You don't ever want to be the person in your organization who hasn't been heard from in days. Be responsive to emails and phone calls. Many organizations now have internal communication platforms that are created to engage employees. Don't be afraid to share your insights on projects or achievements. Participate and share updates in your team's Slack channel or group chat. Doing this allows your colleagues to learn more about you and your skills. It can also provide value to what others may be working on. Also, I can tell you from experience that senior leadership usually reads these postings.

7. **Invest in your colleagues on a personal level.** Even when working remotely, we spend a lot of time at work. Getting to know your colleagues on a personal level is still important when you are working remotely. A member of The Millennial Boardroom goes on virtual walks with a colleague once a week. Don't

underestimate how important it is to still stay connected to your colleagues; being liked is a key component of a successful visibility strategy.

DON'T BE THE BEST-KEPT SECRET.

CHAPTER 4

Level-Up How You Are Seen

> Well-executed visibility = propel to the top
> Averagely-executed visibility = just staying afloat
> No visibility = sinking to the bottom

It's now your job to create an actual visibility strategy and, drumroll please, EXECUTE. I've given you all the tools in this section to identify who you need to be visible to, along with the tactics and actions to make yourself stand out. But I can't execute the steps for you (no one can). This is where the work begins, and you have to own this part if you want to rise to the top. If you want to stay where you are, read this book and don't act. But if you want to advance, then you must get to work.

Think about Coke and Pepsi. Both are well-known brands at this point, but the two companies still make it a point to stay visible; they don't just let the tastes of their drinks speak for themselves. No, both companies spend a lot of time and money to ensure they execute strategies that make them stand out from each other and stay visible to consumers. The same goes for you and your career. *You are the product.* If you don't find ways to be visible, you will send the message that you don't have anything new or valuable to offer. You will communicate that you are ambivalent about getting ahead. If that's the case, why should anyone go out of their way to support you moving ahead? Don't expect others to notice your contributions without drawing attention to them yourself.

Let me be honest with you, some of the actions you need to take to become more visible may make you uncomfortable and feel unnatural if you have never done them before. I have a personal rule that if something I need to do to level up scares me just a little bit (you know that feeling in your stomach you get), that is a signal that I am moving in the right direction.

If you are fearful of taking action to become more visible, come up with your own personal mantra to stop whatever is limiting you. My mantra happens to be the title of this book:

I CAN.
I WILL.
WATCH ME.

I challenge you to come up with your own mantra to say when acting on your visibility strategy feels like it is "too much." As you become more visible, be ready to tackle the new opportunities that you will be presented with and welcome the moments to display your talents and strengths. New projects at work will give you the chance to expand your competencies and make you more valuable to your organization. Be patient and make sure you apply logical reasoning before acting. Sending an email to the chief operating officer to request a meeting because you have some operational recommendations may make you more visible, but it is likely not the right tactic. Think through your moves strategically, then act appropriately.

Before you move on to the next section, I want you to create an actual visibility strategy. If you don't have time to do it right now, block off an hour in your calendar in the upcoming week to complete your strategy. Then, schedule two check-ins—one at the 90-day mark and the other after 180 days—to evaluate how you are executing your strategy. Make adjustments as needed. These steps are essential for accountability.

Here's an easy template you can use to create and review your strategy. You can also access the visibility strategy template at :
www.arikapierce.com/booktoolkit.

Remember, a strategy is only as good as the action that follows.

Visibility Strategy Plan

Stakeholder Name	Power/ Interest	Action/ Tactic	Communication Vehicle	Frequency	Comments

Now that you have a real visibility strategy, I'll tell you some good news. When you make yourself and your value more visible, you will be more empowered for negotiations around promotions and salary increases. We will dive into this in Part Two.

Here's my final advice on being seen: don't be the best-kept secret. Don't wait for others to shine the spotlight on you or invite you to showcase your leadership strengths. Grab that spotlight and point it at yourself! Otherwise, you'll be destined to stay in the dark.

PART TWO

Be Paid & Promoted

Definition of *underpaid:*
paid less than due

> This section will focus on tactics to ensure you are pro-actively positioning yourself for raises and promotions.

My clients and members of The Millennial Boardroom often tell me that they want to make more money and be promoted. After hearing this, I ask them to tell me the title and salary they want. Guess what? Most of the time, they tell me that they need to think about it and get back to me. Here's the thing, I can't help you come up with a plan to make more money or get promoted to a higher level without a clear destination. It's like showing up at the airport and saying you want to go somewhere warm. Does your next career step need to be the final destination? Absolutely not! But you need to clarify where you see yourself advancing next.

In this section, I will tell you how to create a career action plan that will lead you to the salary range and/or promotion you desire. I'm putting my lawyer hat on to say that I make no guarantees that reading this chapter and creating a plan will make you the next senior vice president in your company and increase your salary tenfold. In this section, you will have greater clarity on the steps you need to take to advance, which will help in making career decisions that will lead you on the path of professional success. To put it another way, it's time to get your head out of the clouds and create a real strategy for being paid and promoted if floating through your career and crossing your fingers that things go your way has been your current strategy. "Strategy" is a fancy word for creating a long-term plan *and* executing it, which is what you must do to be promoted and paid more!

YOUR NEXT CAREER STEPS SHOULD SCARE YOU.

CHAPTER 5

Know Your NEXT Career Move

I want to begin this chapter by asking a few questions. Take some time to answer them honestly before we dive in.

1. Are you experiencing career growth?
2. What is the next title or position *you* would like to hold? What about the one after that?
3. What's your timeline for holding these positions?
4. What will you be worth in these next two positions?
5. What will these next two positions mean for you personally? Why do you want them?
6. Who else knows about your desire to move into these positions?

Were you able to answer these questions immediately, or did you tell yourself you needed some time to think about the answers? Do you see a theme here? Perhaps you thought, *I don't know what I want next, but I don't want to keep doing what I'm doing now.* Or maybe you thought, *I'm actually happy in my current career. I don't need to think about what to do next just yet. I'm good.* If you responded in any of these ways, I need you to go back, re-read the questions, and answer them. The questions are hard, so you need to sit with them and think about whether you really want to advance your career. Sometimes, because we don't have the perfect answer, we avoid these types of questions or feel overwhelmed when thinking about the future.

Here's the thing, you don't have to figure out every stop on your career journey. I just want you to think about the next two stops. Also, don't let yourself think too small. Your next stops should scare you a little bit; they should require new skills and pose new challenges. Here's a secret: you are unlikely to see big jumps in your salary without taking on more responsibilities and learning how to solve new problems.

In The Millennial Boardroom, we hold masterclasses every month. The most popular masterclasses are usually about career clarity because, quite frankly, it's easy to get into a career rut. Most people in career ruts want to be paid more and/or promoted to doing something more, but they just can't quite figure out what that "more" looks like. Well, keep reading because I'm going to help you clarify what that "more" is, then create a strategy to get you where you want to be.

STEP 1

For the next work week, spend 10-15 minutes at the end of each day reflecting on your current job. Here are some questions to think about:

1. What specifically do you like or dislike about it?
2. Are you underworked or overworked?
3. How's your relationship with your boss, your team, etc.?
4. Are you learning and being challenged, or can you do your job with your eyes closed?
5. Do you feel connected to and engaged with your assignments, or do you often become bored?
6. How do you feel about the company/organization as a whole?
7. Is there a clear career growth path for you?
8. Has anything happened recently, such as losing out on a promotion or a project?
9. When do you feel unmotivated?
10. When do you feel excited?
11. Analyze your current work performance. What results are you currently achieving?
12. Are you meeting or exceeding performance expectations?
13. What would others say about your value to the organization?

What would others say is your value to the organization? Trust me, if you spend a few minutes each day searching for clarity, this will help to narrow down what's next for you.

STEP 2

Write down all the career-related things that are important to you. Do you value a high salary? A job title? Do you want to have an impact on society? What is your dream job? What stepping-stones will help you get closer to your ultimate career goals? This is the time to also do some research.

When I was still in my corporate position, one of my favorite things to do was window-shop for jobs. Jump on LinkedIn or Indeed and see what out there excites you. Also, look at your current organization's job postings— perhaps a position that wasn't on your radar has been posted. There is no harm in looking at the market. To be honest, if you aren't regularly checking what's out there, you are doing yourself a disservice. I have found that some people treat their jobs like a relationship, so they feel like they are "cheating" if they even browse other opportunities. This is a mindset trap. I want you to stop thinking of yourself as an employee at your company or organization. Instead, see yourself as an individual who is providing a service (i.e., the skill set you possess) to a client. Even though you may not currently be looking for new clients, you also don't want to become so entangled and attached to one client that you don't know what other opportunities may exist to provide your services to new clients. Make sense?

STEP 3

It's now time to have some career conversations. I don't like to use the term "informational interview" because interview sounds like you are job searching. A career conversation is talking to leaders at your organization, in your industry or the field in which you are seeking to change, and asking questions to help you narrow down your next career move.

Here's a template to use when reaching out to someone on LinkedIn for a "career conversation":

Hi [Person's Name],

I was looking for [profession/role] leaders and landed on your profile. I'm impressed with your background and would love to hear more about your career journey as I plan the next steps in my career. Would you be open to jumping on a brief call?

I look forward to connecting.

My number one piece of advice for having a career conversation is to show up prepared. Honestly, I hate when someone asks to "pick my brain," then shows up to a call without any real agenda. Remember, a person's time is their most valuable commodity, so don't abuse it. Here are some questions to ask during a career conversation. Spend time before each call prepping. Remember, don't waste the person's time asking questions that are readily available on their LinkedIn profile or other public forums. Here are a few examples of career conversation questions:

- Can you tell me about your career journey?
- How did you get your current role?
- Can you tell me more about what it means to be a(n) [profession/role]? What does a typical day look like?
- What are the most important skills for this role?
- What should I focus on if I want to get to where you are? What should I learn, or what new skills do I need?
- Are there any specific resources you would suggest?
- Is there anyone else in your network you would recommend I speak to?

TIP: Always send a thank-you email after a career conversation. This is especially important if you met with someone who is outside your network and responded to a cold email outreach. If someone goes above and beyond to help me, I sometimes like to send a small gift of appreciation. My favorite place to do this is www.sugarwish.com (#NotAnAd) because you can select the amount you want to spend on an edible treat, from cookies to popcorn to wine. Sugarwish will email the recipient, allow them to select a gift, then mail it directly to them (this prevents you from having to ask someone for their home address).

STEP 4

Think about the next two years. I like two years because it's easy to visualize. Where do you want to be in your career? If you are willing to go deeper, start also thinking about five years from now. I know, it's hard to see that far into the future, but just give it some real thought. You've done a lot of information gathering, so it's now time to get specific. Write down what is driving you to your targets. This is important because a goal without motivation is eventually null and void.

Based on your goals, I want you to write down the job title (I recommend up to three titles) and salary target that you want for your *next* career move. Perhaps the title is within your organization and clearly mapped out, or perhaps you have identified that your career path has roadblocks at your current organization, which means your next career move is somewhere else. In your notebook or app, write down the following:

1. My next job title is:
2. I will be paid:
3. The current gaps, barriers, or challenges are:

If there are no gaps, barriers, or challenges to getting to the next position, I want you to stop and think about

KNOW YOUR NEXT CAREER MOVE

whether it is the best career move. Growth (and making more money) will usually require you to stretch and step outside of your current comfort zone.

STEP 5

Now, look at the barriers and challenges you listed, then look at the following list. Select three to five action tactics that will help you overcome the barriers and challenges you listed.

CAREER ADVANCEMENT ACTION TACTICS

Ask to lead a project or initiative	Seek feedback from three stakeholders
Identify a problem to solve & present a solution	Have a career-growth conversation with your boss
Take on a stretch assignment	Learn a new technical skill
Create a visibility strategy	Join a professional organization
Seek out a sponsor	Demostrate your value
Make a name for yourself by attending conferences, delivering speeches, or writing articles.	Identify new trends & opportunities
	Document achievements & results
Demonstrate efficiency	

STEP 6

Finally, I want you to set a target date. This is a *realistic* target date to have in mind to achieve your promotion or salary goal. I emphasize "realistic" because the reality is that promotions and salary increases happen at a designated time in many organizations, or there may have to be an opening or organizational shift for you to advance. This is important because as part of this plan and target, you may need to evaluate whether your current organization can support your career advancement goals.

Part of owning your career is having timelines in which you check in with yourself (and others if needed) to help guide you toward what's next. Personally, I understand the need to stay longer in an organization that offers stability over growth. With that said, I am a firm believer that your career is dying if it isn't growing. And sometimes, growth simply can't happen in your current organization.

Before you move on to the next chapter where I will show you how to build out and work your plan, I want to encourage you to complete all six of the steps. Don't skip over the journaling, research, career conversations, etc. Each step is important to make sure you have career clarity beyond just a desire to be paid more or have a more senior-level position. As I shared earlier, many people feel stuck in their careers because they want someone else to do the leading and guiding, but this is *your* career; *you* must own what's next.

"

SMALL STEPS + CONSISTENCY x WINS = MOMENTUM

CHAPTER 6

Create an Action Plan

Answer each question by circling True or False

1. No one cares about your career as much as you do.
   True   False
2. Closing your eyes and coasting is the most danger-
   ous thing you can do for your career.
3. True   False
4. A career action plan will help you set clear priorities and establish a career vision. True   False
5. A career action plan will allow you to evaluate job
   advancement opportunities as they become available to you. True   False

You are one hundred percent responsible for your career.
True   False

If you marked "true" for each statement, then you are
ready to move on to creating your own career action plan.
This is where the rubber meets the road, meaning you are

no longer going to be wishing for a pay raise or promotion; you are now going to have a plan on how to execute.

Your career action plan is essentially a roadmap to where you are going next in your career. This document is for you and you alone, so it's important to put in the right information and adjust it when necessary.

Step 1

Refer to the barriers, challenges, or gaps you identified between where you are now and where you need to be for your next career move.

Step 2

Brainstorm high-level solutions for overcoming the barriers, challenges, or gaps.

Step 3

Write out specific actionable tactics that are aligned with the high-level solutions. Focus on primary tasks that cannot be simplified further.

Step 4

Prioritize the tasks. Decide which ones will have maximum impact, which will take the longest to complete, and which can be executed fairly easily. Also, remove tasks that are unrealistic and/or have low impact.

Step 5

Input your plan into a spreadsheet. I hate staring at a blank screen or sheet of paper and sometimes need something to get me started. If you're the same, then head over to www.arikapierce.com/booktoolkit and download my free career action template.

Step 6

Create a timeline for your tasks and add due dates. Yes, I know this is the hard part, but it's critical for the exercise. Without a time frame, you'll be more likely to deprioritize tasks and forget about them, so you need to set realistic deadlines for yourself.

Step 7

As you look at your tasks, think about the people or resources that can help you. While your career is your own responsibility, it is key to have a support network that helps you get where you want to be faster. You may not need help with every task, but note people, resources, or tools that may be helpful.

> **IMPORTANT NOTE**: After your career action plan template is filled out, I want you to look at it and see if you can identify any Fear Experiments™. Fear Experiments™ is a term used by Judi Holler, author of *Fear is My Homeboy*, to describe anything that is uncomfortable or outside your comfort zone. If you want to be

promoted or paid more, you must have some actionable tactics that will push and stretch you.

In my corporate career, I asked my boss if I could shadow the account manager of one of our clients for ninety days. I had never held a client-facing or operational role (my work was primarily in growth and strategy—big picture stuff), so I wanted to get a better sense of what it meant to manage a client and have daily operational responsibilities. Guess what? It was hard. Clients are temperamental, especially when things are not going right, so account managers must be meticulous. They must also be Excel-savvy which scared the hell out of me. With that said, it was probably one of the best professional Fear Experiments™ I had ever done; it was one of the things that made me stand out as a senior leader who was open to learning and taking a career risk.

Do your Fear Experiments™ need to be as big as mine? No. Just make sure your career action plan requires you to do some things that will push you, stretch you, and ultimately make you stand out.

So, you have your career action plan. Now what? This will come as no surprise, but you will likely not put in the work to actually complete your plan. You're probably thinking, *It sounds like a good idea, but I am too busy right now to get it done,* or *I think relying on the loose plan I have in my head is good enough.* While I don't have raw data, I can tell you that one of the top reasons people do not see pay raises and promotions is because they are not strategic when it comes to their careers (remember, "strategy" is a fancy word for creating a long-term plan and executing it). People assume being ambitious and producing results is enough. Well, unfortunately, it is not. You need to be ambitious AND strategic, and your strategy is in your career action plan.

In my workshops, I often reference the book, *5AM Club*, by Robin Sharma. In the book, Sharma says that ninety-five percent of people are ordinary and five percent are extraordinary. This means there is endless competition at the ordinary level but almost none in the extraordinary zone because to get the results of the top five percent, you need to do what ninety-five percent of people are unwilling to do. If you want to stand out, be promoted, and get paid more, you need a plan. Be the five percent who crush it, not the ninety-five percent who stay where they are.

Staying Accountable

Now that you have a plan, you must commit to working and executing it. Nothing works for those who don't do the work, so be ready to exercise commitment, discipline, and patience.

Step 1

Insert all your action item deadlines into your calendar.

Step 2

Schedule (and keep) a weekly or bi-weekly meeting with yourself to check your progress. Put it in your calendar and don't cancel on yourself.

Step 3

Align yourself with other goal-focused professionals. I suggest getting an accountability partner who is also on a similar path of career advancement. Also, shameless plug, The Millennial Boardroom community is a great place to connect with other like-minded professionals who are focused on career growth.

Step 4

Recognize what's working and celebrate all milestones in your plan. Don't just wait for the raise or promotion.

SMALL STEPS + CONSISTENCY x WINS = MOMENTUM

By planning for the future and setting a specific timeline for accomplishing the things you want to achieve, you will find that your career action plan is effective in ensuring that you never lose motivation along the way.

YOU ARE THE CEO OF ME, INC.

CHAPTER 7

Never Negotiate Against Yourself

You have your plan. You're working it and staying accountable to yourself and your career growth. What happens when it's time to actually negotiate your promotion or pay raise? In this chapter, I will delve into tactics to help you secure your worth (I recognize that every scenario is different). I also want to share that there are many books, experts, resources, and courses that extensively cover negotiations. In this book, I am dedicating one chapter to this topic because I believe you must also place yourself strategically and build a foundation of success in order to be in the best possible position for a career negotiation.

Here are my ten rules for negotiating a pay raise or promotion.

1. **Gather your evidence and "argument" points.** Even if you are not a lawyer, I want you to put on your lawyer hat and pretend that you have to go before a judge to make the case for your promotion and/or raise. This means you need to properly prepare to ensure you have a winnable argument. The three areas you should focus on are (1) past performance, (2) past competence, and (3) future potential. For past performance, gather all your evidence for the value you bring to the organization (more on that in Part Three) and your results. This is where your accomplishments list will come in handy, as well as any accolades from clients, co-workers, other leaders in your organization, etc. Also, this is the time to highlight your work ethic, attitude, adaptability to change, and other soft skills.

    For past competence, you will need evidence of your technical and operational skills. For example, do you have any new certifications that position you for a larger role or more compensation?

    And lastly, you must, must, must make the case for your future potential. Speak to your strategic mindset, capacity to lead, and ability to grow the business. Don't show up to the meeting like an unprepared lawyer, or the judge (i.e., your boss) will quickly see the holes in your case and likely set a new trial date *far* into the future.

2. **Know your numbers.** If you anticipate a promotion or plan to proactively ask for one, do your homework first and know your market value. I personally think that we should be more transparent with our salaries. I don't understand why we are willing to share every other detail about our personal lives, but mum's the word when it comes to how much we are paid. Do some research, gather data, ask your peers in competing businesses, and enlist the guidance of mentors and advisors. For example, if you learn that the competitive pay for your new role would require a $50K increase, which is much higher than your typical five to ten percent pay increase, then you will need to have the right research, data, and justification to make the case for it. Before you start this discussion with your boss, make sure you know (1) your target salary range, (2) your accomplishments, and (3) your accolades. The key here is to overprepare and know your numbers and value *before* asking.

3. **Consider timing.** Asking your boss for a significant raise and/or promotion as they are rushing out the door or going between meetings is not a smart idea. This is a high-stakes conversation. It's not only smart for you to be prepared for the meeting, but you want to give your boss the opportunity to attend the meeting prepared as well. Also, be aware of any current internal obstacles or barriers when considering the timing of your ask. For example, if your company just went through

lay-offs or budget cuts, it may not be the right time to request a raise.

4. **Mindset.** Asking for a raise and/or promotion is not always easy. But if you have worked your career action plan and set yourself up for success by gathering your evidence, then you must be confident that you have *earned* the promotion and/or pay raise you seek. If you go in with the mentality that you don't *deserve* it, you will not be in the right mindset.

5. **Ask for a range.** In my personal experience as both an employee who has asked for a pay increase and a manager who has had employees request pay increases, it's best to ask for a range versus a hard number. Offering a range makes you appear more flexible, but make sure the low-end amount is a big ask so that you will still receive a substantial bump if your boss uses it as an anchor.

6. **Don't ignore other incentives.** I know you want to see the money, but there will be cases when your boss just can't get you as much as you want. If so, what do you do when you aren't ready to walk (yet)? This is when you need to get creative and explore other incentives outside of your direct salary. This could include more paid time off, tuition or professional development reimbursements, bonuses, or even an upgraded job title.

7. **Practice the conversation scenarios.** Asking for a raise and/or promotion is a high-stakes conversation, but so

many people just wing it. Don't make this mistake. Ask your mentor or even a friend to role-play with you and explore a few different conversation scenarios. How will you start the conversation? How will you address any pushback? How will you explain your market value and amplify your accomplishments? I suggest making a list of every reason why your boss may not think you deserve a raise or promotion and create a counterargument for each issue. Planning and practicing will help ensure that you remain confident, maintain control of the conversation, and stay focused on reaching your goal.

8. **Be ready for next steps**. In a perfect world, when you asked for a raise and/or promotion, your boss would say, "I'll call HR right away!" However, in many cases, your boss will explain that the budget has already been spent or that he or she will need some time to make it happen. If your boss gives you either of these types of responses, be ready to establish next steps. First, get clarity on what you need to do between now and "later" to ensure you receive the raise or promotion you are requesting. This is especially important if you are unable to get a raise or promotion because your manager thinks you have not earned it yet. In this scenario, be prepared to find out exactly what you need to do to earn the raise or promotion you have asked for. For example, would they like for you to take on any additional responsibilities or work on a special project? Also, be sure you establish a timeline so that you are

clear about when you need to check back and report on your progress so that you are on track to get your raise and/or promotion in a reasonable time period.

9. **Send a follow-up email after the conversation.** Whether your conversation went the way you wanted it to or not, always send a follow-up email after the conversation. This is to document the full discussion, especially if your boss gave you feedback on areas you needed to focus on to make the promotion or raise happen. Also, this is good information for HR or the finance department if your boss quits, is fired, or moves to a new role shortly after your conversation (you never know). This email is also important because your boss will likely forward it to the other approvers (i.e., their boss, HR, etc.) so that they have all the information they need to make a decision about your raise and/or promotion. If you ask for a raise *without* sending this email, then your boss will have to summarize your case for you. Let's face it, they're just not going to do as good of a job as you will. Being able to "speak" to the convo is not enough—having actual documentation is key for this type of professional communication. On the next page, I provide a sample template of what your email should detail.

TIP: Write out this email *before* the discussion but don't send it. This will help you prepare for the discussion, then you can update it after the actual conversation.

10. Be aware of empty promises. I'll be honest, I know a lot of people who deserved a promotion or raise, followed each of these steps, but never got what they asked for. They were told to "give it some time" or that they would get their raise or promotion as soon as some event happened. While I do believe in being realistic with your ask and exercising patience, you have to also recognize an empty promise. If there is no foreseeable path forward, you owe it to yourself to explore new opportunities. If not, you will be holding yourself back.

Template Email:

Hi **[Boss' Name]**

Thanks for your time today. As we discussed, it has been **[amount of time]** since **["my last promotion or significant salary adjustment," OR "I was hired,"]** and I would like to revisit my salary now that I'm contributing much more to the company. I've been researching salaries for **[proposed job title]** in the **[industry name]** industry, and it looks like the mid-point is around **[mid-point salary from your research]**. So, I would like to request a raise to **[target salary range]**.

I've been working very hard to find ways to contribute value to our company. Here are some of my accomplishments over the past several months:

[Accomplishments]

- **Activity → result**
- **Activity → result**
- **Activity → result**
- **Activity → result**

And here is some feedback I've received from clients and coworkers over the past several months. Their feedback speaks louder than anything I could say:

[Accolades]

- **[Client or co-worker's name]—"Quote" or general feedback documented in email or survey**
- **[Client or coworker's name]—"Quote" or general feedback documented in email or survey**
- **[Client or coworker's name]—"Quote" or general feedback documented in email or survey**

I believe these accomplishments and feedback show that my work merits an elevated role and higher salary, and **[target title and/or salary]** seems well-aligned to the current market, as well as with the additional value I have added to our company since my current salary was set.

Do you need anything else from me?

Thanks again for your time!

[Alternative if a date was set to revisit]

Hi **[Boss' Name]**

Given that your feedback was that the timing isn't quite right for a [raise or promotion], I want to be ready when it's time to revisit our conversation.

Can you review the areas for growth that I captured from our discussion and the timeline? Also, I'd like to plan to check in on **[date]** so that we can continue this discussion and monitor my progress as I work toward my goal.

Thanks for working with me on this!

Final Advice

Here's my final advice on getting paid and promoted. Think of yourself as a business (remember, you are the CEO of Me, Inc.). When a business wants to expand, it creates a growth plan, breaks it down into small chunks (usually by quarters), then tracks and monitors the progress. You must do the same thing for your career. Don't just sit around waiting for "what's next" to happen to your career. Instead, get clear on your next role and start coming up with a plan for how to get there.

Most organizations are not going to pay you more or promote you for being stagnant. You have to showcase your value and results, then connect the dots to show how you will positively impact the organization in the future. When you do this, you will be in the driver's seat of a negotiation and have a far better chance of getting to where you want to be next. With that said, I am a firm believer that growth doesn't happen in comfort zones, so you must also be aware that you may have to look for a new company or organization if you want to make a major jump in your career. And frankly, that's okay. Be loyal to yourself and your own career growth first. The most important thing to remember is that *you* are in control of your career. So, where do you want to go next?

DON'T UNDERESTIMATE THE WEIGHT OF A POWERFUL, PROFESSIONAL BRAND.

PART THREE

BE VALUED

Definition of *undervalued*:
not valued or appreciated highly enough

> *This section will focus on how to ensure your strengths are known and promoted by YOU.*

How well can you articulate your value? Would you give yourself an A? What about a B? Would you perhaps give yourself a D or even an F? I'll be honest, this is the section of the book that I was most excited to write because it addresses one of the most overlooked and underused career tools. It is the area where so many struggle, and it's a topic that comes up over and over again in The Millennial Boardroom community. If you gave yourself a low grade on how you articulate your value, don't worry because you are not alone. So many people complain that they are not appreciated enough or valued at work, but when I ask them to speak about their values, superpowers, or strengths, I'm often told to give them a few minutes to think. Better yet, they say something incredibly vague like, "I work really hard."

In this section, I want to show you how to be a valued rock star at work and claim your professional fame. There is value in being visible, and it has nothing to do with being brilliant or lucky. You just have to be focused on delivering and promoting yourself as someone whose contribution is valuable and understood. Think about it, if your organization doesn't know who you are and doesn't understand what you can do, then how can they possibly utilize you to your maximum capabilities?

I know that standing out may not be something you are incredibly excited about when it comes to your career, but it is easier than you think. And you don't have to be an extrovert to reach rock star status. Don't underestimate the pull of a powerful, professional brand as you take your career to the next level. I'm going to make you a star!

WHAT DO PEOPLE SAY ABOUT YOU WHEN YOU ARE NOT IN THE ROOM?

CHAPTER 8

Boss Up Your Brand

When I am hired by companies and organizations to do professional development workshops, I give them a range of topics I can speak on. Any guess about the number one most requested topic? It's personal branding. This tells me that a company wants its employees to think and strategize about how they are perceived. Employers want you, as a future leader, to align your career trajectory with their brands because a professional brand speaks to your value.

Before we get into the nuts and bolts of how to boss up your brand, let me tell you something. More specifically, Jeff Bezos (you know, one of the richest men in the world) says, "Your brand is what people say about you when you are not in the room." While this might not be a big deal to you, know that most major decisions about your career are made when you are not around. Decisions about whether to hire, fire, or promote you will likely be made behind closed doors; your goal is to ensure that your brand consistently speaks volumes among key decision-makers and stakeholders throughout your career. Essentially, your brand is:

- Your reputation
- How you're seen by others
- What people can expect from you

Building up and bossing up your brand means that you understand your strengths and differentiating qualities, as well as how to leverage them to set you apart in your company and career. Knowing your strengths and how to use them will put you in direct control of how others perceive you instead of letting them decide who you are and what you stand for. Additionally, understanding your unique qualifications is important for your career because when you clearly understand what sets you apart, you can position yourself as a top performer worthy of recognition. You can position yourself on the front line and proactively seize exposure opportunities. Building your boss brand will require work, but you will gain the ability to confidently advocate for yourself and truly own your accomplishments in return. You will have an established strategic and internal support network that recognizes your value and propels you to reach your career goals. Most importantly, you will increase your value, impact, and leadership while making conscious efforts to advance your career.

So, how do you build this rock star brand? Here are the steps:

Step 1: Find out where your brand currently stands

You already have a brand. Agree or disagree? Well, everyone has a brand whether they realize it or not. The difference is that many people have a default brand that is built by design. With that said, before you start designing your brand, you need to know how you are already "branded" in the minds of others. To get a baseline of your brand, I want you to do a couple of things.

- **Ask your network**. This is the first thing you should do. Identify five people you trust—colleagues, managers, mentors, sponsors, etc.—and ask them to share the answers to the following questions. I'll state the obvious: asking someone to answer these questions is not easy, and sometimes the feedback can be hard to receive. I guarantee that ninety-five percent of people will choose to skip over this step of establishing their baselines. But remember, this is about attaining the five percent extraordinary mindset and doing things that ninety-five percent of people don't want to do.

> **TIP:** Set up a SurveyMonkey or Google Forms survey so that everyone can answer the questions honestly and anonymously.

Personal Brand Feedback Questions

- What are my three greatest strengths?
- What are my three greatest opportunity areas?
- How do people describe me when I am not around?
- Name one to two things I am particularly skilled at.
- Provide general feedback on my personal brand, image, or reputation.

- **Google yourself.** Now, there are lots of caveats here. If you have a common name like Steve Smith, a lot of non-relevant information will probably come up in a search. However, it's good to be aware of this because it's one of the reasons some people decide to use a middle initial professionally. If you have a unique name, nothing may come up when you look yourself up (this is not necessarily a good thing). No matter what your name is, I want you to spend a little time on Google to see what turns up. Many people see their LinkedIn profile in the top ten search results. This is a good time to see how accurate and up to date the information is. Based on what you found (or didn't find), how are you perceived online? Is there anything on the internet that would negatively impact your professional reputation?

- **Review your social media accounts**. I'm sure I don't have to explain to you the importance of protecting your brand on social media. Today, we see people in trouble left and right because of things they tweeted years ago or posted on Facebook, Instagram, etc. Recently, I had a client, who was job searching at Fortune 500 companies, post a number of pictures of herself wearing "nightwear" on her public Instagram page. Immediately, I brought it to her attention and shared that people don't want to see their current or future leaders in their underwear. She disagreed, but I feel firmly about this.

- **Analyze your annual review and accomplishments list**. Many times, when we receive our annual review, we look for any negative feedback, sign it, and move on. As you think about your brand, this is a great time to pull your last few annual reviews, especially if they were done by different managers, and look for common themes or traits that were written about you. It's also a good time to look at your accomplishments list. To date, what are some of the things you are known for? What do people compliment you on?

- **Review your image.** If anyone tells you that your image doesn't matter when it comes to your brand, they are lying to you. How you visually "show up" and communicate creates an impression of who you are and your overall value. It may not seem fair to be judged on areas such as how you look, but it's reality. Write down your current image and what your style says about you. Think about how people "experience" you through your appearance, attitude, behavior, and communication style.

Now that you have all this information, I want you to do some self-analyzing. What are you currently known for? How do people describe you when you are not in the room? If your existing brand is not communicating your value and distinctiveness as a leader, you are not alone. The goal is not just to have any brand but to have a powerhouse leadership brand that is valued and known.

Step 2: Create your unique value proposition

Set a phone timer or stopwatch for forty-five minutes and do an uninterrupted brain dump to answer the following questions. There are no wrong answers, but the goal is to be one hundred percent honest.

- What am I passionate about?
- What are my strengths?
- What are my weaknesses?
- What sets me apart from others in my field?
- What do I want to be known for?
- What's the first thing I want to have pop in someone's head when he or she hears my name?
- What strengths do others see in me?

- When working on a team, what roles do I tend to fulfill?
- When faced with an overwhelming obstacle, what are my "go-to skills" to solve it?
- What is the most successful project that I've ever tackled, and what made me successful?
- Which of my skills motivate or excite me?
- Which of my skills have I mastered but would rather not use every day (i.e., burnout skills)?
- What skills and strengths are going to be most useful in achieving my career goals?
- What skills am I missing?
- What skills would I like to practice but haven't had an opportunity to build?

After your brain dump, take a break. This type of work isn't easy. Once you are ready, review your answers and start to zero in on three to five traits and/or characteristics that you want your brand to be defined by as you position yourself as a rock star leader. I don't want you to create a brand that will keep you where you are professionally. Identify the brand traits and characteristics for your bossed-up brand, meaning the ones that will represent you when you reach the next tier of your career. For example, if you are a mid-level professional, your brand should not be about *doing* the work; it should be about *leading* the work.

TIP: In her book, *Women of Influence*, Jo Miller shares some key descriptors that define brands at different career stages. Review these as you start to think about the right type of characteristics and traits for your bossed-up brand.

Entry-Level Brands

- Valued contributor
- Team player
- Tactical executor
- Get sh!t done
- Specialist
- Go-to person

Mid-Level Brands

- People motivator
- Project leader
- Team catalyst
- Strategist
- Results driver
- Fixer
- Process improver
- Customers' champion
- Subject-matter expert
- Innovator

Senior-Level Brands

- Leader who develops leaders
- Culture catalyst

- Big-picture leader
- Makes big things happen
- Turnaround architect
- Transformational leader
- Dealmaker
- Thought leader
- Visionary

After reading these words and phrases, which resonate with your unique value proposition? If you were up for a raise or promotion, what types of statements do you want to be said about you when you are not in the room? Remember, your brand and value proposition should always be evolving. For example, if you are currently known for getting things done, start to think about how you can evolve into a business transformer or strategic influencer.

Step 3: Create your leadership brand statement

Now that you have more clarity about how you want to be experienced and spoken about, it's time to pull it all together in a leadership brand statement. This is a short statement (I recommend seventy-five words or less) that you can refer to and use as needed to speak to who you are and why YOU matter. This is not your job title or role in your organization; it is a statement about YOU. If you get stuck, try to fill in these blanks:

*"I want to be known for being_____ so that I can deliver
_____."*

Here's an example that one of The Millennial Boardroom members recently shared with the community:

"I want to be known for being innovative, collaborative, and strategically results-oriented so that I can deliver superior financial outcomes for my team and our organization at large."

Also, as you think about your statement, ask yourself if it describes something your company values. Does it highlight your strengths? Does it fuel your passions?

I know this is a hard step in the process, but it's a critical one to take as you proactively make an effort to be valued. If you are not able to articulate your value, then there should not be an expectation that others should know your strengths, contributions, or results.

Still need some motivation? Here are a few more examples of leadership brand statements that I think are powerful.

> *I'm a committed team player and effective relationship builder. Leaders, peers, team members, and clients recognize the passion and enthusiasm I've consistently demonstrated in successfully driving change through motivating, coaching, mentoring, and training teams.*

Innovation is in my blood...I seek to find ways to adapt when needed and disrupt when possible. For the past 15+ years, I have been at the forefront of digital evolution and transformation as an intrepid business strategist, thought leader, and functional operator, and called on to develop solutions and technologies that have enabled stronger customer engagement, retention, and loyalty.

I'm a modern, fearless, digitally-driven, and globally savvy brand/business leader with over 15 years of experience representing two of the most exciting, influential consumer brands in the world. I live for opportunities to deliver game-changing, digital, and physical global marketing programs that deepen consumer connections, accelerate revenue, and drive brand growth.

I'm a business and marketing leader focused on delivering epic results through innovative, fun, and highly differentiated go-to-market activities, while empowering people and teams to do the best work of their lives.

And here is mine!

I am a driven and high-energy former corporate executive who inspires and motivates emerging leaders. I achieved early success in my corporate career and now leverage my professional experiences to position new leaders for their peak performance.

Developing professionals is my skill. Leadership coaching is my passion. Creating the next generation of high-performance leaders is my motivator.

Step 4: Live up to your brand statement

Now that you have your brand statement, it's time to share it and live up to it. Think about specific ways you can demonstrate your brand and set yourself up to be seen and valued. For example, if your brand is to be valued as a thought leader for your team or organization, make sure you are keeping up with trends and changes. Are you a hub of knowledge? Have you ever volunteered to speak on a company webinar panel or author a blog post? You must make it easy for people to connect the dots on the value you bring as a leader in your organization.

Step 5: Practice your brand statement

While at a conference recently, I heard a story about two men in an elevator headed up to the same office at the headquarters of a bank in London. One man was a high-profile senior executive at the organization, and the other was a young analyst who had just joined the company. The young analyst, of course, recognized the senior executive, but the senior executive had no idea who the analyst was because they had never had any face-to-face interactions.

As the elevator started to move, the executive asked the young man what he did at the bank. The young analyst was ready; he mentioned his role as an analyst but said it was his goal to lead a telecom investment team in southern Asia. He also noted the ties between his country of origin and how he would be the ideal candidate to lead the team. Once he finished, do you know what happened? The senior executive asked for the young analyst's business card and stated that he would pass it on to the head of the subcontinent investment team. Then the executive said, "If you don't hear from him, let his office know I personally told you to call."

Think about yourself in a similar scenario, would you be ready to share your brand statement with a powerful stakeholder at a moment's notice? Trust me, you never know what's around the corner, so this is an important step that should not be skipped.

IF YOU WANT TO
BE VALUED; YOU
NEED TO HAVE
AN EDGE.

CHAPTER 9

WHAT'S YOUR SECRET SAUCE?

I am going to tell you a secret, then you can tell me yours. Organizations value effective leaders. Leadership is not a job title or position; it is an action. If you want to be valued at work, you must be seen as a leader at *every* point in your career. There are *appointed* leaders, and there are *accepted* leaders; being the former doesn't guarantee that you'll be the latter.

So, what's your secret sauce as a leader? Review the "40 Secret Sauce Qualities" listed over the next several pages and write down the ones you recognize in yourself currently, as well as the three you would like to see in yourself one year from now. Also, feel free to tweak these phrases to make them more specific. Spend some time thinking about how and why this secret sauce quality sets you apart from your peers and colleagues? For example, lots of people can say they see the big picture, but what are *you* doing to showcase this as your secret sauce? When I worked for a publicly traded company, I always listened to the earnings calls and found ways to showcase the fact that I was doing this to senior leaders in the company. I always read press releases and sent notes over to a team leader who'd had a big win even if I didn't know them. When I had one-on-ones with my boss, I asked about strategic initiatives and shared articles about industry changes and trends with my colleagues and on LinkedIn. This was my secret sauce, and it led to me becoming the senior vice president of growth and strategy at that company.

Here's the bottom line: If you want to be valued, you need to have an edge. Nobody can be you; that is your distinct competitive advantage. Here is another secret: Your secret sauce is oftentimes right in front of you, and it is not always a technical skill. In his book, *The Undercover Edge: Find Your Hidden Strengths, Learn to Adapt, and Build the Confidence to Win Life's Game*, Derrick Levasseur says, "Sometimes, in our society, we try and do what everyone else is doing to be successful when, in actuality, what we should be doing is using what's successful to us." So, as you think about how to be valued, consider this: What comes naturally to you that amazes others? That's your secret sauce!

40 Secret Sauce Qualities

1. Self-motivated
2. Thinks strategically
3. Thinks critically

4. Strives for continuous improvement
5. Communicates with transparency
6. Delivers effective speaking presentations
7. Gives open, honest, and direct feedback
8. Active listener
9. Stays calm in difficult situations
10. Breaks down complex information into simple terms
11. Stays positive and constructive during difficult conversations
12. Focuses on results
13. Acts decisively
14. Exudes energy and determination
15. Maintains a positive attitude
16. Takes charge and assumes responsibility
17. Has excellent organizational skills
18. Takes risks
19. Exudes honesty and dependability
20. Earns respect
21. Collaborates
22. Communicates
23. Shows empathy
24. Inspires and empowers others
25. Manages up, down, and across
26. Rallies people to achieve a common goal
27. Relates work to the organization's goals
28. Motivates people and aligns them around team goals
29. Ensures team spirit is upbeat
30. Sets clear expectations

31. Trusts others to do their jobs without micromanaging
32. Enables others to be successful
33. Allows people to learn from mistakes
34. Empowers others
35. Acts as a strong advocate for those they manage and mentor
36. Gives credit where it is due
37. Attributes successes to those who contributed
38. Encourages others to do their best
39. Ethical
40. Emotionally in control

Adapted from Woman of Influence: 9 Steps to Build Your Brand, Establish Your Legacy, and Thrive (McGraw-Hill) by Jo Miller.

THE #1 BLOCKER TO CAREER GROWTH IS FEAR.

CHAPTER 10

What Would Your Career Be Like If You Weren't Afraid?

As you start to read this last chapter, I hope that you are ready to get to work on being seen, paid and promoted, and valued. It's going to require growth and courage, and in my line of work as a leadership coach, the number one thing that holds people back is fear. They fear failure. They fear trading security for the unknown. They fear what others will say or think. Is fear a factor in your career success? I want you to spend some time thinking about this, then write down any fears you have when it comes to taking the actions that have been outlined in this book.

If you weren't afraid to fail, what would your career be like? How many times have you avoided opportunities that would have given you visibility? How many times were you silent in a meeting because you felt your comment or question would come off as "stupid", when in fact it could have added immense value to the discussion?

So, let's talk about some common fears:

Fear of Failure

I believe that most people approach failure the wrong way. Failure is part of the journey to success. Failure is inevitable, and it is a learning opportunity. If you look at any of the most successful people in the world, they all have massive stories of failure. The fear of failing makes people not go after a promotion or take on a stretch role or assignment. I tell my clients and The Millennial Boardroom members all the time that they should be most afraid when they are comfortable because that's a sign that they are not stepping outside of their comfort zone to grow and thrive.

Fear of Rejection

Is fear of the word "no" holding you back? When reading Part Two of this book on how to be promoted and paid, did some of the steps make you feel a little uneasy because you feared your request might be rejected? I know this is a common thought among people, especially Millennials. But here's the thing, if you don't ask, the answer will always be "no" by default. Also, I have found that even if the answer is "no," just making the request shows the level of control you want to have over your career and demonstrates professional maturity, which will set you up for success in the future.

Fear of the Unknown

Growth does not happen in comfort zones. We often convince ourselves that things are "good enough" because we are uncertain what moving into a higher role, changing jobs, switching careers, etc. would look like. Start to dip your toe into unknown territory from time to time to get more comfortable with being uncomfortable. Remember those experiments to exercise your fear from chapter five? Which of those can you act on today?

Fear of Being Out of Your League

I hear so many people talk themselves *out* of the next career opportunity all the time. Perhaps their company posted a job that they want to apply for, but they fear they don't have enough experience or assume that so-and-so would definitely get it over them. My advice is to use the time and energy spent talking yourself out of applying to strategize on how your experience and secret sauce are relevant and make you the right fit for the position.

Fear of Loss of Freedom

When it comes to your career, you may find that you don't want to take on a promotion or additional responsibilities because you fear the loss of your freedom. That promotion might include new duties, different working conditions, more hours, more pressure, and more stress. But it's in our nature to focus on the potential negatives rather than the positives. There are always going to be tradeoffs. Yes, career advancement typically comes with more responsibility, but it can also position you for more future growth opportunities that lead to higher compensation.

Fear of Judgment

I recently did a career training session in The Millennial Boardroom on the importance of presentation skills for career growth. A lot of people fear public speaking because they don't want to be judged, and so they pass on opportunities that would otherwise help them to be seen and valued. You can't let the fear of judgment control you. To be honest, you are likely underestimating your confidence and exaggerating how much others will evaluate you.

Fear of Something Bad Happening

Are you avoiding career advancement because you're afraid that something catastrophic will happen? If so, you are also avoiding the possibility of something great happening. I don't believe in being reckless when it comes to your career, but sometimes you must take risks. Before you decide not to apply for that promotion, ask yourself, *what is the worst that could happen?* It's usually not as bad as you make it out to be!

Fear of Being Greedy

Are you someone who wants to make more money but doesn't want to talk about it because you don't want to appear greedy or unappreciative? If you are seeking to be paid your value and worth, you can't let this fear cause you to low-ball yourself or accept less than you deserve. If you follow the techniques discussed in Part Two and enter these conversations with knowledge and confidence in your results and worth, then let go of any fears and discomfort around talking about money.

Fear of Not Being Perfect

My motto is "done is better than perfect." When it comes to taking action regarding your career, I see many suffer from perfectionism; they miss job application deadlines because they are still tweaking their resumes. Or they don't reach out to connect with a key stakeholder because they want to make sure the email is "just right." These are excuses fueled by fear, and they will hold you back from making progress.

Fear of Disappointment

Are you afraid of being disappointed? You think, *This amazing opportunity can't possibly be as good as it seems.*

You've got a glowing review from your manager, but now you're paralyzed—afraid of making a mistake and letting her down. This fear is often the reason we avoid career advancement opportunities, but not taking a chance often leads to more regret than any disappointment over taking the chance ever could.

Fear of Growth

Are you currently working in an environment that will propel your growth? This is a hard question for many people to answer. If they say "no," then the natural follow-up question is, "what you are going to do to change that?" I'm not advocating that you quit your job, but it's important to know whether or not your current environment supports your growth. If not, start to strategize ways to change that either within your organization or outside of it.

Leadership expert John C. Maxwell has what he calls "growth environment" statements to help you identify if you are in an environment to grow. I find that many people want to advance their careers, but they don't take necessary actions because they are comfortable playing it safe. Growth equals change, but many of us fear change.

Read the following ten statements to assess your current work environment by answering "true" or "false" to each.

1. Others are *ahead of me.*
2. I am continually *challenged.*
3. My focus is *forward.*

4. The atmosphere is *affirming*.
5. Failure is not my *enemy*.
6. I wake up *excited*.
7. I am often out of my *comfort zone*.
8. Others are *growing*.
9. People desire *change*.
10. Growth is *modeled and expected*.

How did you do? If you answered "false" to more than five statements, then your current environment is likely hindering your growth. Next, write an honest review of where you are in your career and work environment.

I want to close out this chapter and this book with one of the ways I tackle my fears. I recite a mantra any time I feel doubt, procrastination, or uncertainty within myself. I say:

I CAN.
I WILL.
WATCH ME.

I CAN.
I WILL.
WATCH ME.

SUMMARY

Thank you for sticking with me to the end! I am proud of you, and you should be proud of yourself. Remember that ninety-five percent of people are comfortable being comfortable and ordinary; they don't read books like this one. If they do, they definitely don't finish, and most importantly, they don't take action because it's simply uncomfortable! I know we have covered a lot of topics in these ten chapters, so I am going to summarize the actions that you need to take to move forward so that you don't skip anything!

Part One: Be Seen

1. Check your mindset on how you see yourself. In your journal, answer the question on page 11. Remember to be honest.
2. For one week, take ten minutes at the end of each day to reflect on who you are as a leader at work. Remember, leadership is an action, not a title or position.

3. Start to narrow in on who needs to "see" you in order for your career to advance. Complete the stakeholder analysis on pages 16-17.
4. If you don't regularly have skip-level meetings with your boss' boss, schedule one and use the questions on page 26 to drive your agenda.
5. Using your stakeholder analysis and the exposure tactics from page 34, complete your visibility strategy. Schedule two check-ins—one at the 90-day mark and the other after 180 days—to evaluate your progress.

Part Two: Be Paid & Promoted

1. Answer the questions on page 63 about the current stage of your career.
2. Complete all the steps outlined to create your career action plan.
3. Come up with your accountability strategy. Remember, SMALL STEPS + CONSISTENCY x WINS = MOMENTUM
4. Set a timeline for your next raise or promotion; start to prepare for your promotion/salary conversation with your boss or manager.

Part Three: Be Valued

1. Find out where your brand currently stands—how do others currently experience you?

2. Identify your unique value proposition and create it into a leadership brand statement. Once you are comfortable reciting your leadership brand statement, start living up to it.

3. Review the 40 secret sauce qualities on pages 112-114 and write down the ones you recognize in yourself currently, as well as the three you would like to see in yourself one year from now.

4. Complete the exercise on pages 122-123 to evaluate if you are currently in a "growth environment."

5. Write an honest review of where you are in your career and work environment. Include any fears that are holding you back from growth.

Ready for more?

As I've shared throughout this book, there is an amazing community of ambitious professionals in The Millennial Boardroom (no, you don't have to be a Millennial to join). If you are looking for an affordable way to access career coaching, networking, help with accountability, and a career-growth-focused community, then I invite you to join us.

More information can be found at: www.themillennialboardroom.com.
I hope to see you in the Boardroom!

ACKNOWLEDGMENTS

In 2018, I wrote *The Millennial's Playbook to Adulting* as a creative outlet while I still worked full-time. I had no idea that the book would lead to a career pivot and that I would start my own leadership development company, Piercing Strategies, which focuses on helping organizations strengthen and diversify their leadership pipelines.

There are so many people who have supported me over the past four years that I am almost afraid to name them individually for fear of forgetting someone important. That said, I want to thank everyone who has supported me in this new career endeavor—I appreciate you buying my books, coming to my workshops, following me on Instagram and LinkedIn, and sending me notes to say I helped you move forward and grow in your career. THANK YOU! THANK YOU! THANK YOU!

I also want to thank my village of family and friends who are always my #1 promoters. I will definitely not name names because there are too many to list. An extra special thanks to my parents, Ada and James, my grandmother,

ACKNOWLEDGEMENTS

Rosie, my sister, Adey, and fiancé Andre (I promise, your 10% is coming)!

There are so many more to name. I don't want to get myself in trouble, so I will stop there and just be grateful to all my family and friends.

And lastly, for anyone who has ever felt like they were being looked over, not paid their worth, and not valued for their contribution, this book is for you, especially my fellow Black women.

Thank you for reading, and I truly hope you found some real strategies to take control of your career and navigate yourself to the top!

ABOUT THE AUTHOR

Arika Pierce is a Leadership Coach, attorney, author, and speaker, and the CEO/Founder of Piercing Strategies., a leadership development consulting firm that works with organizations to strengthen and diversify their leadership pipelines.

She leverages her fifteen years of experience in corporate leadership positions to deliver solutions and programs that help professionals grow and thrive as leaders.

Arika is a sought-after speaker whose interactive speaking style effectively engages audiences. She often mixes content with humor and leaves audiences with actionable and tactical tools to own and advance their careers.

Arika believes that beyond empowerment, her programs strengthen individuals to show up more fully and authentically and recognize their leadership identity.

Through her keynotes, coaching, workshops, and books, she supports the next generation of leaders in their journey.

Arika holds a JD from The George Washington University Law School and a BA in political science from Louisiana State University.

> *My whole adult life has been a series of sink-or-swim moments. Meaning, I've had to make quick decisions to succeed through my own efforts or fail. Luckily, each time I chose to swim, which meant I've had to take a lot of risks and step outside of my comfort zone in order to succeed. These experiences have shaped my life and led me to break barriers that I didn't even know were possible.*

Connect with Arika
LinkedIn: https://www.linkedin.com/in/arikapierce/
Website: www.arikapierce.com
Instagram: @arikalpierce

Join us in The Millennial Boardroom Community
www.themillennialboardroom.com

REFERENCES

Coleman, Harvey, *Empowering Yourself: The Organizational Game Revealed* (AuthorHouse, 2010)

Holler, Judi, *Fear Is My Homeboy: How to Slay Doubt, Boss Up, and Succeed on Your Own Terms* (Greenleaf Book Group Press, 19)

"Fear Experiments™" is a term used by Judi Holler, author of *Fear is My Homeboy*.

Levasseur, Derrick, *The Undercover Edge: Find Your Hidden Strengths, Learn to Adapt, and Build the Confidence to Win Life's Game (Sourcebooks, 2018)*

Miller, Jo, *Woman of Influence: 9 Steps to Build Your Brand, Establish Your Legacy, and Thrive* (McGraw-Hill, 2019)

Made in the USA
Middletown, DE
21 September 2022

10897416R00080